D1244625

Social Intelligence Skills for Government Supervisors/Managers

Stephen J. Sampson, Ph.D.
John D. Blakeman, Ed.D.
Robert R. Carkhuff, Ph.D.

HRD Press, Inc. • Amherst • Massachusetts

Published by: HRD Press, Inc.
22 Amherst Road
Amherst, MA 01002
800-822-2801 (U.S. and Canada)
413-253-3488
413-253-3490 (fax)
www.hrdpress.com

ISBN 0-87425-910-X

Production services by Jean Miller
Cover design by Eileen Klockars
Editorial work by Sally M. Farnham

Table of Contents

Acknowledgment

The intervention skills model analyzed in this manual has been adapted from the Human Resource Development (HRD) model developed by Dr. Robert R. Carkhuff, Chairman of the Board of Directors, Carkhuff Institute of Human Technology.

This HRD model is copyrighted and any use of this material without the written permission of the copyright owner would be a violation.

We gratefully acknowledge the generosity of Dr. Carkhuff for his permission to adapt this material. Two resources provided the major framework for this manual:

- Blakeman, J. D.; Pierce, R. M.; Keeling, T.; and Carkhuff, R. R. *IPC: Interpersonal Communications Skills for Correctional Management.* Amherst, MA: HRD Press, Inc., 1977.

- Blakeman, J. D.; Pierce, R. M.; Keeling, T.; and Carkhuff, R. R. *IPC: Interpersonal Communication Skills for Corrections—A Training Guide.* Amherst, MA: HRD Press, Inc., 1977.

Preface to the Trainee

This is a skills-oriented course: no "shoulds" or "oughts," but rather practical, applicable skills that are immediately useful. The program is realistic. It is not designed to take issue with the fundamental management skills you have or will learn in your formalized training or that you receive from the tutoring of more experienced leaders. It is designed to complement both of those: to **add** to your skills base so that when you **choose** to use it, it will be there.

Overview of the Learning Plan

The learning plan is both simple and systematic. First, the trainer will **Tell** you what the learning module is all about. Second, he or she will **Show** you the skill that will be learned in the module by demonstrating its use. Third, he or she will then have you learn the skill by **Practicing** it in a role-play activity. Fourth, and last, you will have **Input** into the learning both by evaluating the role player and then having an opportunity to discuss the activity thoroughly and give your thoughts and ideas based on your observations of the role play.

Like any training, failure can be programmed as well as success. The key to success is your willingness to participate fully in the written exercises, role plays, discussions, and sufficient practice. Good luck!

Introduction to the Intervention Skills Model

During this training segment, your trainer will preview the intervention skills model. He or she will explain that the skills to be taught come from the experiences of managers just like yourself. He or she will then outline the model:

INTERVENTION MODEL

THE APPLICATIONS: CONTROLLING BEHAVIOR

1. Handle Requests
2. Make Requests
3. Reinforce

THE ADD-ONS: COMMUNICATIONS

1. Respond
2. Ask Questions

THE BASICS: SIZING UP

1. Arrange
2. Position
3. Posture
4. Observe
5. Listen

EXPLANATION

Traditionally, the training given to government managers has been aimed at their heads—it was filled with theories and ideas. Sure, there was some skills training, but that was usually in computer or other technical areas. Another thing about the training was that it was almost exclusively concerned with the technical aspects of managing. While these are obviously legitimate concerns, this orientation doesn't take into account the fact that managers spend much (if not most) of their time interacting with people—and with each other.

Managers traditionally have been trained to get the job done, but not necessarily to get along with people effectively. More important, they haven't been trained in how to get supervisees to do what the manager wants them to do without a hassle, which is what the job is really all about.

The training program is an effort to change that orientation. It's based on work done by trainers and researchers over the past fifteen years. It's known as human resource development. It's based on a careful study of the skills that truly effective managers demonstrate. Techniques for identifying those skills have been developed and now there are techniques for teaching others, like you, how to acquire and use those skills.

This training program is designed around the human resource development model. A model is like a road map: it shows you where you're going. As you can see from the diagram on the previous page, the model has three major sections.

The Basics The **basics** are pre-management skills that give you information that helps you decide what action to take in any given situation. Another name for the basics is **sizing-up skills.**

The Add-Ons The **add-ons** are communicating skills that will help you get a supervisee to explore and share information with you. These skills are the key to finding out what's really going on in a situation.

The Applications The **applications** are skills that help you control behavior in a respectful way—so that **you** get what you want done with minimal hassles.

During this training program, you'll get a chance to learn about and practice all of these skills.

NOTE Throughout this book, you will see blocks indicating "VIDEO." A DVD was developed as an additional training tool to accompany this book; it is available for purchase by going to our Web site, www.hrdpress.com or www.sotelligence.com.

PRACTICE　Think back on your own experience of being managed. You've probably had bosses who you thought did a good job in managing you, and others who you felt did a poor job. Think about the good bosses. What qualities or skills did they demonstrate that made them effective in managing you—that made them successful in motivating you to do a good job? List those qualities and skills below.

_____

_____

_____

_____

_____

_____

_____

_____

_____

Section I

The Basics:
Sizing Up the Situation

The basics are sizing-up skills that help you know what's happening in any situation. Sizing up helps you avoid costly mistakes and maximizes the chances that your decisions and actions will be effective and accurate. Sizing up works because it gets you ready to use information to manage and often to prevent problems. Using the basics is always appropriate because every situation you experience needs to be sized up.

INTERVENTION MODEL

THE BASICS

Sizing Up the Situation

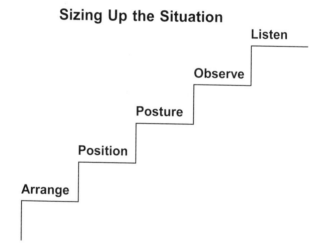

FIVE BASIC SKILLS Sizing up any situation involves five very basic skills:

1) Arranging
2) Positioning
3) Posturing
4) Observing
5) Listening

Why basic?　The word *basic* is important here. The five skill areas are basic and fundamental to everything you will learn in Sections II and III of this manual—and to everything that you actually do on the job. You cannot hope to communicate safely and effectively with a person or persons until you have used these skills to size up the situation.

You cannot hope to control people unless you have first sized up the situation. By learning to make continual use of the five sizing-up basic skills, you can maximize your chances of making the right response in situations where a wrong response could be very costly.

The five basic skills are cumulative in that each new skill builds on each previous one. For example, positioning effectively means that you should already have arranged your environment; posturing yourself effectively means that you should already have arranged your environment and be in an effective position; observing accurately means that you should already have arranged your environment and gotten into an effective position and posture; and so on. In other words, you don't simply use one skill at a time. Instead, you size up a situation by making maximum possible use of all five basic skills.

Getting ready　In general, of course, the skilled manager always systematically sizes things up in his or her workplace and the people in it. Here are some ways a manager sizes things up in his or her work environment upon arriving to the workplace:

- Walks around the area of responsibility to see who is in and what they are doing
- Checks in with secretary/support staff for messages and e-mails
- Determines if there are items that need priority attention

It is in this final phase of preparing for work—and in the actual duties that follow—that the manager puts the five basic skills to maximum use.

PRACTICE Why do you think that sizing up the situation is important?

_____

_____

_____

_____

If you were to think about your responsibility prior to arriving at the workplace, what would you be thinking about?

_____

_____

_____

_____

Which of the basic skills do you think would be most helpful for you to get that information?

_____

_____

_____

_____

Arranging

How you arrange, or order, the environment in which you manage or supervise contributes to your goal achievement. If you are highly skilled regarding your interpersonal management skills, the arrangement of the environment will be somewhat overshadowed in importance by your skill level. However, if you regard your people management skills as only moderately effective, as is the case with most managers, then this is an area in which you should expend real effort.

When we examine the behaviors of highly functional professionals, one dominant trait they display is that they place a lot of significance and importance on details. Arranging sub-skills focus on the details of the environment.

INTERVENTION MODEL

THE BASICS

Sizing Up the Situation

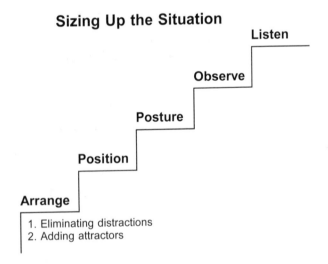

Arrange
1. Eliminating distractions
2. Adding attractors

Arranging means eliminating from the environment anything that might distract you or the person who you are supervising or with whom you are interacting. A second goal of arranging is to make the environment pleasant, not stressful, by adding attractors.

Eliminating distractions. The first principle of arranging is eliminating distractions. Most people have worked in an environment where there were many distractions. Remember what it was like to try to perform your job effectively when you worked in a distracting environment? For both you and your supervisee, outside noises, uncomfortable chairs, and an uncomfortable room temperature can divert your attention and deplete your energy so that more time is required for each task and errors occur more frequently.

Imagine the work environment where you manage others. Are there noises that can be eliminated? Can phone calls be intercepted? Is furniture reasonably comfortable? Does the placement of furniture create a barrier? Or is it best to simply remove yourself and the person with whom you are talking from the distracting work environment and talk with them in a quiet conference room? Eliminating those distractions is important to successful communications and interactions.

ARRANGING means eliminating from
the environment anything that might
distract you **or** the person whom you are
supervising or with whom you are interacting.

VIDEO

"Eliminating Distractions: The Wrong Way and the Right Way"

PRACTICE

List some distractions you experienced when you were in the presence of your supervisor or manager and communication was important.

_____

_____

_____

_____

Adding attractors. The second sub-skill of arranging is adding attractors. Following the elimination of distractions, you might consider actually adding *attractors* to the environment. You can enhance your work environment in order to manage and communicate more effectively. Providing privacy and comfortable furniture, and having refreshments may all facilitate your efforts. Your best standard is probably the one you would establish for yourself.

ARRANGING means adding
enhancements to the environment
that may lead to reduced stress and
more effective communication.

PRACTICE   List the characteristics of a present or past environment that either contributed to reducing your stress or facilitated your ability to communicate with others.

_____

_____

_____

_____

Positioning

Positioning means putting yourself in the best possible place to see and hear individuals or groups. This helps you see and hear what is necessary in order for you to carry out your duties and to keep minor incidents from becoming major ones.

The three parts of positioning are:

INTERVENTION
MODEL

THE BASICS

Sizing Up the Situation

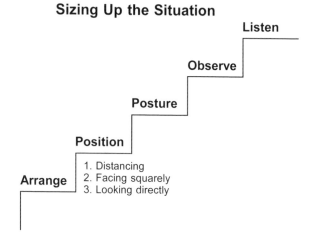

Listen

Observe

Posture

Position

1. Distancing
2. Facing squarely
3. Looking directly

Arrange

Physically positioning yourself in relation to an individual or a group is very important in managing people.

There are several different principles or activities that you may feel are important to effective positioning. The three basic parts of positioning that we will focus on in this section are establishing an appropriate distance, facing squarely, and looking directly.

As an effective manager, you need to position yourself where you can see and hear problems. Being in a good position helps you to know just what's going on and, therefore, to resolve issues before they become major problems. In addition, positioning helps you deal with people who think that when they are not being observed, they can live by the rule "We'll get away with as much as we can—or as much as you let us." Of course, it's impossible for you to be everywhere at once, yet the more you use positioning skills to see and hear, the less likely it is that supervisees will get involved in things that are against policies.

Positioning also communicates interest to supervisees, which gives them a feeling of security and that you care about their well-being.

Now let's look at the three positioning skills or procedures outlined above.

PART 1 OF POSITIONING   **Distancing.** The first principle of distancing is to be able to observe and listen to what you are managing. Of course there will be many situations where you can't observe supervisees (e.g., when you are talking to a supervisee on the phone) or listen to them (you can see their actions but can't hear what's being said).

On the other hand, if supervisees are in your office or talking with you in the hallway, choose a distance that enables you to observe and listen to them more effectively.

POSITIONING means distancing yourself close enough to see and hear the people you manage if the situation allows for it.

VIDEO   **"Distancing: The Wrong Way and the Right Way"**

PART 2 OF POSITIONING   **Facing squarely.** Facing squarely, or fully, ensures that your position gives you the most effective line of vision. Your left shoulder should be lined up with the left boundary line of the area you are watching, and your right shoulder should be lined up with the right boundary line of the area you are watching. When you move your head to either side so that your chin is right above either shoulder, you should be able to see the entire field for which you are responsible.

POSITIONING means facing a person, persons, or area squarely.

See everything

Sometimes the size of the area for which you are responsible (for example, a set of cubicles) makes it impossible to remain in one position. In this situation, you must rotate yourself so that by successive movements, you will squarely face all the areas or persons you're responsible for. Facing fully helps you size up a situation. You can see best when you are directly facing people, and when your goal is communication with people (Section II), this also lets them know that you are open to hearing them.

VIDEO **"Facing Squarely: The Wrong Way and the Right Way"**

PART 3 OF POSITIONING

Looking directly. When positioning yourself, you should look directly at the area or person(s) you are managing. Unless you look directly, you will not be on top of the situation even if you are in the right position and are facing squarely. Looking directly at a group often involves looking at their eyes. When questioning people, for example, you will be able to get important clues by observing their eyes and their facial expression closely.

In addition to the information you can get, your direct look tells people that you are confident and are not threatened. However, looking directly doesn't mean you should get involved in a staring contest, but many people believe that a person who won't look you in the eyes is being deceptive.

POSITIONING means looking directly
at the area and person or people
you are managing.

Eye contact may also be the best way of communicating interest. People become aware of our efforts to make contact with them when they see us looking directly at their faces. Of course, looking directly at people will also provide you with valuable information about them. People who keep shifting their eyes while talking to you signal that, at the very least, they are either uncomfortable with you or with what is being said. This kind of information is important in sizing up a person's mood or emotional state.

You must also keep in mind that "direct" eye contact may be threatening to some people based on the individual or circumstances (cultural differences).

VIDEO   **"Looking Directly: The Wrong Way and the Right Way"**

PRACTICE   You probably have many work stations (cubicles, office, conference room). Think of some of these stations. Describe where you would position yourself to size up the situation.

Station: _____

Position: _____

_____

Station: _____

Position: _____

_____

List two situations in which you think it would be a good idea to look a supervisee directly in the eye.

1) _____

_____

2) _____

_____

List two situations in which you think it would *not* be a good idea to look a supervisee directly in the eye.

1) _____

_____

2) _____

_____

ROLE-PLAY ACTIVITY

Supervisee	Manager	Group
Role plays for 20 seconds.	Positions for 20 seconds. - Distancing - Squaring - Looking Directly	Critiques manager for appropriateness of his or her position.

Posturing

Using good posture means holding your body in a way that shows strength, confidence, interest, and control. When you appear strong and confident, people will believe that you are strong and confident.

THE BASICS

Sizing Up the Situation

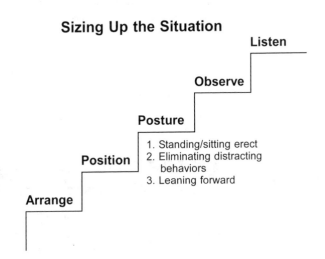

Listen

Observe

Posture

Position   1. Standing/sitting erect
2. Eliminating distracting
   behaviors
3. Leaning forward

Arrange

Your posture—how you carry yourself—tells people a lot. It can make a person think that you're confident of yourself or that you're really pretty worried about what might happen. Your aim, of course, should be to show your real confidence.

As with positioning, there are several ways in which you can use posturing when you are sizing up the situation. Here we'll focus on three specific procedures: standing/sitting erect, eliminating distracting behaviors, and leaning forward.

The way in which the first two procedures show confidence should be obvious. When you stand erect and get rid of distracting behaviors, you let people know that you're in full physical control—control not only of your own body, but of the whole situation.

And that's essential! Many people will try to intimidate any manager who doesn't look as if he or she is confident about what he or she is doing. If a person thinks he or she can scare you, you're in real trouble. Any manager without respect is open to embarrassment and abuse.

Example For example, there was one manager who was known to avoid the first sign of trouble. Supervisee's felt really uncomfortable with this person as a manager. But while most of the supervisees simply didn't trust this person, some supervisees were always taking advantage of that manager and getting what they wanted.

Eventually there were reports of supervisees sleeping while at work, abusing computer time, and arriving late to work. The final blow was a situation where a questionable behavior between a male supervisor and a female co-worker put the whole department in a liability situation.

By standing erect and eliminating distracting habits, you show your strength and that you mean business.

The third part of the posturing skills outlined here, leaning forward, can also show confidence by reinforcing the idea that all your attention and potential energy is committed to job performance. But leaning forward, as you will see in Section II, can also help you communicate your interest when you choose to provide any human service. Used in this way, such a posture says to a person, "I am inclined to listen, to pay attention, to be interested, to help."

All right, let's take a closer look at the three parts of posturing already outlined.

Standing/sitting erect. We all know how important erect posture is. You probably heard it as a child, and you definitely heard it if you were in the armed services: "Stand your full height," "Be proud, stand up straight," "Stick out that chest," and "Pull in that gut."

Erect posture takes muscle tone and practice. Look in the mirror and check yourself out. Are your shoulders straight? Is your chest caved in? How do you feel? Ask someone else for his or her reaction. Which way does he or she experience you as stronger and more confident?

POSTURING means standing/sitting erect to show strength and confidence.

VIDEO **"Erect Posture—Sitting or Standing: The Wrong Way and the Right Way"**

Eliminating distracting behaviors. A person who can't stand steady is seen as not being at ease with him- or herself or others. Biting nails, foot-tapping, and other distracting behaviors do not communicate confidence and control. However, standing stiff like a board doesn't communicate confidence either. A good rule of thumb to avoid stiffness: You should not feel tension in your body after you have eliminated distracting behaviors.

POSTURING means eliminating all distracting behaviors.

VIDEO **"Eliminating Distracting Behaviors: The Wrong Way and the Right Way"**

PRACTICE List some distracting behaviors that **other people** sometimes show.

_____

_____

_____

_____

What are some distracting behaviors that **you** sometimes show?

_____

_____

_____

_____

PART 3 OF POSTURING **Leaning forward.** Your intention here must be to communicate interest and concern by shifting your weight forward so that the people become more aware of your "inclination" to communicate and supervise them with respect. Doing this communicates "moving closer" without actually moving you much closer or making any physical contact. Since this position shows you to be more alert, it also gives you more control over the situation. Lean your weight away from another person. What do you experience? Probably a "laid-back" sort of remoteness. You're simply not as involved.

POSTURING means leaning forward to show that your attention is really focused.

VIDEO **"Leaning Forward: The Wrong Way and the Right Way"**

	Supervisee	Manager	Group

ROLE-PLAY ACTIVITY	**1)** Talks for 30 seconds.	**1)** Positions:
		  - Distancing
		  - Squaring
		  - Looking
		    directly
		
		Postures:
		  - Sitting erect
		  - Eliminating
		    distracting
		    behaviors
		  - Leaning
		    forward
			1) Observes manager's ability to maintain positioning and posturing behaviors for 30 to 60 seconds.

	2) Talks for 60 seconds.	**2)** Manager repeats above.	**2)** Group repeats above.

Observing

Observing is the ability to notice and understand individuals' and groups' appearances, behavior, and environment. Careful observation of actions will tell you most of what you need to know about people, their feelings, and their difficulties. The four steps in observing are:

THE BASICS

Sizing Up the Situation

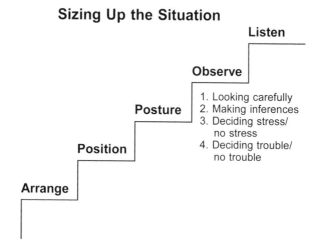

Listen

Observe

Posture

1. Looking carefully
2. Making inferences
3. Deciding stress/ no stress
4. Deciding trouble/ no trouble

Position

Arrange

Looking carefully at behavior, appearance, and environment. A *behavior* is a nonverbal cue provided by something that a person does while conscious and active. For example, you might observe any or all of the following behaviors: two people holding hands, one person bumping another, a person looking in a store window, a person wringing his or her hands.

An *appearance* is a nonverbal cue that a person might display even if he or she were unconscious or dead. For example, you might observe the following appearances: one person is African American, one person didn't wear clean clothes today, one person is an older person, one person is wearing a T-shirt and shorts.

17

Environment includes the physical settings people live/work in (e.g., neighborhoods, homes, workplace) and the people they live with and relate to (e.g., friends, family, and co-workers). It also includes environmental experiences that have influenced their lives (e.g., education, military, vocation, and culture).

What is she doing?

How does she look?

Where is she? And with whom?

When observing a person, you should ask yourself questions such as "What's she doing right now?" (behavior), "What are the important things about how she looks?" (appearance), and "What's important about where she is and who she's with?" (environment). For example, a supervisee named Jim Barker has been coming to work late (behavior), his clothes are wrinkled and hair unkempt (appearance), and he is separated from his wife and three children, living in an apartment alone (environment).

OBSERVING means looking at behavior, appearances, and environment.

Once you're able to answer these questions, you're ready to draw some inferences about a person.

VIDEO "Observing Behavior, Appearance and Environment"

PART 2 OF OBSERVING

Making inferences about feelings, relationships, energy level, and values. Inferences are the initial conclusions you come to as the result of observing people. You take in visual cues related to a person's appearance, behavior, and environment. These cues are really clues that show you something about a person's feelings, relationships, energy levels, and values. The more observations you make, the more inferences you can draw and the more accurate these inferences will be. Inferences are important because they provide valuable information that increases your ability to manage another person or predict that person's future behavior. Referring back to the example on the previous page, Jim may be feeling down (feeling) due to his separation from his wife and children (relationship), and his poor grooming may be due to low motivation (energy) due to not seeing his children (values being a parent).

OBSERVING means making inferences about feelings, relationships, energy levels, and values.

Making inferences about feelings

The manager can use his or her observing skills to draw inferences about how an individual or an entire group of people is feeling. Knowing how a person is feeling is critical in determining where a person really is. For example, you might use the feeling word *happy* to describe a person who is exercising and smiling. For a person who is pacing while wringing his hands, you might apply the feeling word *tense.* You might use the term *uptight* to describe a group of people who are tightly clustered and speaking with one another in a well-guarded, hesitant manner.

What feeling word would you apply to the following examples?

1) A supervisee is sitting at his desk, head hanging down, clenching his fist, and staring straight ahead.

Feeling Word: _____

2) Sitting at a desk, a supervisee is holding up a photograph of a small child while pointing to it and smiling broadly, laughing and occasionally waving the photograph around.

Feeling Word: _____

VIDEO | **"Inferring Feelings and Why"**

Making inferences about relationship

Besides being aware of the nonverbal cues that indicate the feelings of a person, a supervisor can further increase his or her effectiveness in management by looking for cues that indicate the nature of the relationship between him- or herself and the people he or she supervises, and among people in general. The relationship between the manager and his or her supervisees, and people in general, serves as a good indicator of future action.

A supervisee who has a good relationship with you may take directives from you without difficulty or conflict. Conversely, one who has a poor relationship with you may be hard to motivate to follow your directives.

Is he positive, negative, or neutral about others?

In general, you can categorize relationships and feelings as positive, negative, or neutral. People who do things to make your job easier (e.g., keep you informed) probably have or want to have a positive relationship with you. A person who always tried to hassle you (e.g., uses abusive language, refuses to obey rules) doesn't have or doesn't want to have a positive relationship with you. When a relationship is a neutral relationship, it is purely business with minimal emotional commitment—positive or negative (e.g., business transaction between you and a salesperson in a store).

Example Among people, relationships of power are critical. It's common for people to form their own group with a leader. Knowing the relationship within and between groups is crucial. For example, a group of supervisees has developed an office clique. One of the supervisees within the group has had a couple of run-ins with you. He is also the informal leader of the group. You begin to notice that some of the supervisees in his group are now acting differently toward you. This situation could obviously affect your ability to manage these other supervisees if you start to have a negative relationship with them.

PRACTICE List two behaviors and/or appearances that would tell you that two people have a negative relationship with you:

1) _____

2) _____

What might result from these behaviors and/or appearances?

_____

_____

List two behaviors and/or appearances that would tell you that two people have a positive relationship:

1) _____

2) _____

Making inferences about energy level

High? Low? Moderate?

Energy level tells us a great deal about how much and what type of trouble a person can or may cause. For example, people with a low energy level are reluctant to initiate anything. Many people have a low energy level. They look and act defeated. Their movements are slow, their heads hang down, and every move seems like an effort. These individuals may spend a good part of their time being nonproductive. People with moderate energy levels actively engage in most activities (playing, working, talking, eating), while high energy people not only participate in all that is required, but also make use of physical fitness programs and many other activities. The danger of high energy, of course, is that this energy needs to be used constructively so that it does not become a source of problems.

While it is important to observe basic levels of energy, changes in energy level are even more critical. Energy levels are usually constant for people, except at special times (weekends, special sporting events, holidays). Abrupt changes from high to low to high may indicate trouble (to self or others).

PRACTICE

List two behaviors that show a high energy level:

1) _____

2) _____

List two behaviors that show a low energy level:

1) _____

2) _____

List two special times that might cause energy levels to change:

1) _____

2) _____

VIDEO **"Inferring Energy Level and Why"**

Making inferences about values

It is also important to understand as much as possible about a person's values. Here is where observing the environment comes in. Every person has three basic environments: the place where he or she lives, the place where he or she works, and the place where he or she learns. In each of these settings, the actual "environment" will include not only physical materials but people—the people a person "hangs with." You can learn a great deal about people by carefully observing their environment. A general rule is: What people give their energy to is of value to them: the more energy given, the higher the value.

What interests a person?

Values are the ideas (religious beliefs), things (automobiles, jewelry), and people (spouse, children) they have a strong bond toward.

Knowing what a person values has real implications for effective managers. When you know what a person wants and doesn't want, you've got an edge in supervising that person when necessary.

PRACTICE

List three of *your* important values:

1) _____

2) _____

3) _____

VIDEO **"Inferring Values and Why"**

23

The reasons for your inferences should be **visual cues** related to *behaviors, appearances,* and *environment.* Inferences stand the best chance of being accurate if they are based on detailed and concrete observations (black hair, scar on cheek, shaking their fist, with three other males in break room) rather than on vague and general ones.

PRACTICE

Read the following incident carefully. Be ready to give reasons (descriptions of appearances and behaviors) for some inferences you will be asked to draw.

Incident

12:00 p.m. Lunch Time. You observe four supervisees in the lunch room. You notice one is standing, addressing the other three who are sitting. He is pointing his finger at one of the three. He has a scowl on his face. When the supervisee he is pointing at tries to speak and one of the other supervisees tries to say something, the standing supervisee looks directly at them and cuts them off.

Write down the feelings of the standing supervisee, his relationship to the group, and his energy level. Cite reasons for your inferences. **Note:** The reasons should be descriptions of the appearances and behaviors demonstrated that support your inferences.

Feeling (angry, scared, happy, sad):

_____

Reason: _____

_____

Relationship (positive, negative, neutral):

_____

Reason: _____

_____

Energy Level (high, moderate, low):

_____

Reason: _____

_____

PART 3 OF OBSERVING **Deciding whether things are stressful or not stressful for a given person or persons.** Once you've been on the job for some time, you get to know how individuals tend to function through observation. One person is easy-going and hardly ever hassles you or others. A second person always looks like he or she is mad at the world. A third always seems to be feeling sorry for him- or herself. Your observations and the inferences you've drawn can help you determine whether a particular person is in a "stress" or "no stress" condition **for him- or herself** at any point in time.

OBSERVING means determining if
things are stressful or not stressful.

In determining whether things are stressful or not stressful for a given person or group at a given time, compare your present observations with any past ones and/or with any comments that other people may have made about these people. For example, you may observe an individual arguing loudly with another person. He may even be making mild threats of one kind or another. If this is normal behavior for this person, you probably need to exercise only the usual amount of caution. But if the appearance and behavior of the angry person are highly unusual or abnormal for him, you'll know it's a potentially troublesome situation.

Example Normal behavior for Jim Barker, the individual mentioned previously who is separated from his wife and three children, is to smile when you initially see him and to be very animated (using his hands while talking). His normal appearance is to keep his hair neatly combed, to be washed regularly, and to have his clothes pressed and creased perfectly, with shoes polished. Since his separation from his wife and children (environment), his behavior and appearance has changed (i.e., not smiling very much, not animated, and clothes and shoes not kept up).

VIDEO **"Decide Stress or No Stress"**

PART 4 OF **Deciding if there Is trouble or no trouble.** This
OBSERVING decision should be based on your observations and your knowledge of a person or persons. With your knowledge of a person, you should be able to generate criteria that will be useful in making this decision (e.g., "abrupt and/or major changes in behavior and/or appearance could mean trouble," "a supervisee who has a history of being positive has a greater likelihood of managing stressful events in life despite changes in behavior and appearance").

OBSERVING means deciding whether it's a "trouble" or "no trouble" situation.

VIDEO **"Decide Trouble or No Trouble"**

Observing appearance and behavior is usually the quickest and most accurate way to detect whether or not a given individual is really having a problem. People may be very reluctant to talk to you about problems. Your observations will allow you **Important to** to anticipate problems so that you can prepare for **know** their possible impact on other people, you, other supervisees, or the people themselves. **Remember, nonverbal behavior accounts for 60 percent to 90 percent of any spoken message.**

PRACTICE Your instructor will guide the group through role-playing activities that will give you more practice in using the skill of observing.

1) Feeling: _____

   Reason: _____

   _____

2) Relationship: _____

   Reason: _____

   _____

3) Energy level: _____

   Reason: _____

   _____

4) What knowledge or principles do you have that would apply to the situation?

   _____

   _____

5) Stress or no stress? _____

   _____

6) Trouble or no trouble? _____

   _____

ROLE-PLAY ACTIVITY

Supervisee	Manager	Group
1) Describes setting.	**1)** Positions Postures	**1)** Pays attention.
2) Role plays for 60 seconds (tells story about where he/she grew up).	**2)** Observes behavior, appearance.	**2)** Writes own answers to behavior, appearance, feelings, relationship, energy level, value, mood of supervisee.
3) Provides nonverbal cues (behaviors) while conveying his/her story.	**3)** Infers feelings— relationship, energy level, values.	
	4) Describes mood.	

Listening

Listening is the ability to hear and understand what people are really saying. Listening helps you hear the signals from people while things are still at the verbal stage so that you can take appropriate action to manage situations before they get out of hand.

INTERVENTION MODEL

THE BASICS

Sizing Up the Situation

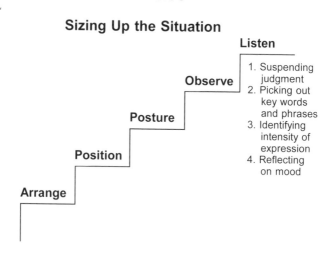

Listen
1. Suspending judgment
2. Picking out key words and phrases
3. Identifying intensity of expression
4. Reflecting on mood

Observe

Posture

Position

Arrange

VERBAL CUES AND SIGNALS

People often go through a verbal stage before the action begins. If you can hear the signals, you can cut off any trouble before it really begins. Listening involves your ability to hear and accurately recall all the *important* verbal cues used by people—*important* because of implied signals of trouble or problems. The danger may be an individual's intention to get into trouble, harm another person, etc.

In the workplace, complaints are common, of course, but they're also important. An effective manager listens to complaints and recognizes when a familiar cue is uttered in a new tone or when a complaint arises from a normal, uncomplaining person. An effective manager listens especially for changes: silence when there is usually noise or noise when there is usually silence. Once again, the manager asks him- or herself the question: "Is there trouble here?"

GETTING READY TO LISTEN

As indicated, you should get ready for listening by using the basic arranging, positioning, posturing, and observing skills whenever possible.

Arrange

Arranging your environment to eliminate distractions and to make it pleasant will help you focus on the person talking.

Position

A good position will obviously help you hear better.

Posture

Posturing, while perhaps less important in terms of listening for good management, is essential when you're listening to a person who really wants to talk to you. Your posture can signal to the person that you're focusing all your attention on him or her.

Observe

Finally, your observing skills cannot always be used to promote better listening. For example, you may overhear something that people are talking about around the corner. But when possible, visual observations help you understand the implications of what you're hearing. A person who sounds angry but turns out to be leaning back in his chair and grinning may have only been telling a story to others; an individual whose angry voice fits with his tense, uptight appearance presents quite a different situation.

One more preliminary thing: You can't listen effectively to people if you've got other things on your mind. If you're thinking about home or other job responsibilities, you may miss a lot of what is said and what it really means. You've got to focus on the person to whom you're listening—and this takes a good deal of concentration. You can work to develop this kind of concentration by reviewing what you're going to do and whom you're going to see before you begin work. Then you'll really be ready to start using the four specific procedures that skilled listening involves.

Suspending judgment. This is very difficult for anyone to do, but especially for those in charge. In many circumstances, you have just witnessed a violation of workplace policy. If, however, your goal is to get more information about what happened, you will need to get people to open up more. Suspending judgment, at least temporarily, can assist with that.

It is still hard at times to listen without immediately judging because many people with whom you must deal get defensive (e.g., clam up, get upset, or become vague) very quickly when you, as a manager, try to talk with them. Despite this, it will severely hurt your management efforts if you do not suspend judgment because you will never hear the real verbal cues you need in order to get more information or to assist someone.

LISTENING means **suspending your own judgment** temporarily so that you can really hear what is being said.

All complaints sound the same after a while, but they are *not* all the same! Some are just the normal whines and gripes, while others are real warning signals of potential problems. Just let the message sink in before making any decisions about it. Of course, certain situations call for quick action, but if you develop your nonjudgmental listening ability, you will hear better and be able to take appropriate action more quickly when necessary.

VIDEO · **"Suspending Judgment: The Wrong Way and the Right Way"**

Picking out key words and phrases. There are key words and phrases to listen for. Here are a few: *downsize, jerk, hate, quit.* Of course, everything you hear must be considered in terms of who said it. Some people are always sounding off. In addition to the key words you hear, it's important to add your observations and knowledge of the person who said them.

LISTENING means **picking out the key words and phrases** such as *the suits* or *company man.*

PRACTICE List some words and phrases that signal danger or trouble in your particular environment.

Example "Cuts" _____   Clerical _____

_____   _____

_____   _____

VIDEO **"Pick Out Key Words and Phrases: The Wrong Way and the Right Way"**

Identifying intensity of expression. Statements are made with varying intensity (high, moderate, and low). The louder and more emotional a statement, the more intense it is. But loudness and emotion are not the same thing. A wavering voice, for example, signals a lot of emotion, even though it may not be loud. A statement that is either loud or emotional but not both is most often of moderate intensity.

Volume?
Emotion?
Intensity?
High,
moderate,
low?

A statement that is loud and is empty of emotion is usually of low intensity. High intensity statements are very real signs of danger.

VIDEO **"Identify Intensity of Expression: High, Moderate, or Low"**

LISTENING means **determining
whether the intensity of a person's
speech is high, moderate, or low.**

PART 4 OF **Reflecting on what the mood is.** Is the person's
LISTENING mood positive, negative, or neutral? Normal or
abnormal? Why? *Mood* here means, at a very
simple level, what people are feeling. One question you may ask to determine mood is "What
kinds of feelings are being expressed or implied
(positive, negative, or neutral)?"

Another question you want to answer is "Is
this mood normal or abnormal for this time and
place?" Sure, there are always exceptions. For
example, a person can say "I'm going to hurt
somebody" quietly and without emotion, yet still
mean it. This is why it is so important to know as
much as possible and to continue to observe and
listen for other cues.

LISTENING means **determining whether
a mood is positive, neutral, or negative,**
and whether this mood is **normal**
or **abnormal.**

Reasons When you answer the question, "Is this normal or
abnormal?" you should try to formulate the reason
why this is the case. *Normal* means "as it usually
is." This can apply to one person as well as to a
large group of people. People are usually quite
consistent in their behaviors in their various
settings—they are creatures of habit. For
example, it's not normal for people to be real quiet
when they are among others who are being very
noisy and animated.

VIDEO **"Identify Mood: Positive, Negative, or Neutral"**

33

ROLE-PLAY ACTIVITY	Supervisee	Manager	Group
	1) Describes setting 2) Role plays person for 20 to 30 seconds 3) Provides verbal cues for conveying information (high, moderate, low) 4) Defines mood (positive, negative, neutral) 5) Determines mood (normal, abnormal) 6) Why?	1) Positions Postures Observes Suspends judgment Says nothing 2) Pulls out key words 3) Identifies intensity 4) Rates person on #2 through #6 (yes/no)	1) Positions for paying attention 2) Writes own answer 3) Rates manager on sizing-up skills

Summary of the Basics

You have recently heard rumors that Joe Smith, one of your supervisees, has been leaving work early, but not taking leave time. Your office is not in the area of the building where Joe works. He therefore can leave without you being aware of it.

Joe is a good employee who is not known for breaking the rules. You also heard that he is having problems with his adolescent son. Joe is a single parent and has sole custody of his son.

Joe has been leaving between 2:30 p.m. and 3:00 p.m., but the days vary. There is not a consistent pattern.

You decide to go where Joe parks his car the next five days. You go every day around 3:00 p.m. You notice on two of the days, his car is not in the employee parking area. Inferences are better based on direct observation.

Arranging Skills   You bring Joe into your office the following week. You close the door and forward your phone to eliminate any distractions.

Positioning Skills   You come out from behind your desk and ask Joe to sit in a chair that allows you to position and posture. You pick a position 3½ feet from Joe, body squared, looking directly.

Posturing Skills   You say to Joe, "I've noticed your vehicle has not been in the parking area after 3:00 p.m. on Tuesday and Thursday, but you have not been taking leave. What's going on?" You maintain an erect posture while sitting, keep your body still, and lean slightly forward.

Observation Skills   You **observe** that he is very nervous and his shirt is wrinkled (not normal for Joe). Your inferences are based on your observations.

Listening Skills You keep your body still and tell yourself to suspend your judgment. You also tell yourself to pay close attention to what he says and how he says it.

All right, you've had a chance to learn the five basic skills you need to size up a situation—to manage your job and people more effectively. You've practiced arranging, positioning, posturing, observing, and listening. But as you know, there's far more to being an effective manager than being able to size things up. There will be times when you choose to manage by communicating. You'll want to defuse a troublesome situation or get important information. There may even be times you choose to become more involved.

In the second major section of this manual, we'll consider the skills you need to communicate effectively. The skills in this section, while often secondary to other management skills in some situations, are absolutely essential when dealing with many tense situations—situations where strong feelings may get out of control or are interfering with your ability to understand what you need to. Sizing things up just lets you know what's happening and what may happen. To manage things for the better—and that's what effective management requires—you need to add on communication skills.

THE ADD-ONS

1. Respond
2. Ask Questions

THE BASICS

1. Arrange
2. Position
3. Posture
4. Listen
5. Observe

Section II

The Add-Ons:
Communicating with People

Add-on skills help you open up communication with people. They provide you with the ability to get another person to tell you more about what he or she knows or thinks. You'll find the add-on communicating skills invaluable whenever you need to get more information about a situation or when you **choose** to become involved.

The two add-on communicating skills are:

THE ADD-ONS

Communicating with People

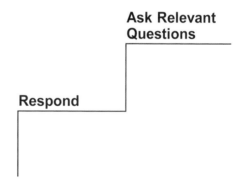

**Ask Relevant
Questions**

Respond

It's been said that the only thing worse than a person with seniority who thinks he or she knows it all is a new person who's sure he or she knows it all—but doesn't. You may be new to management, or you may have some management experience. Whatever your situation, you've probably run across managers who are very rigid in their approach. They see little need for compromise. To these managers, anything less than "throwing the book" or "telling it like it is" is weak

37

and the reason the system doesn't work. There's a lot of logic in their thinking, but only up to a point.

Example　One manager found this out to his considerable embarrassment. A new manager was in another manager's office. The new manager was venting his frustration at the situation (from Section I) involving Joe Smith leaving work early without permission. He relayed to the older manager that if he was Joe's manager, he would have terminated him on the spot. He states the following: "The problem with the organization is that employees believe they can get away with anything just because they have problems at home."

The older manager remained calm as the new manager vented. All of a sudden, the new manager's cell phone began ringing. As he talked on the phone, his face became pale. He appeared speechless. As he got off the phone, the new manager said, "I've got to leave right now. It's my wife and she says that our four-year-old may have a serious medical problem. I've got to leave."

Older Manager:	You've got to be scared.
New Manager:	I've been telling my wife that the kid is always whining about not feeling well. Now I feel like such a jerk.
Older Manager:	You're probably feeling guilty because you were sure the child was complaining about nothing and your wife was just overreacting.
New Manager:	I do right now. I probably need to go home, but my boss Bill says I'm new and the job requires you to keep your personal life and your work life separate.

Older Manager:	You are afraid to ask Bill if you can leave? What makes you think he wouldn't understand that this situation is unique?
New Manager:	Because I told him my job always comes first.
Older Manager:	Well I know he would understand this situation is different. Do you want me to talk with him? I've worked with him for years.

Skills Make the Difference

Well things worked out. The new manager talked with his boss Bill about the situation. His boss told him, "If something this serious takes place, you should attend to it right away." He added, "If something like this happens in the future, you do what you need to do, but just let me know beforehand. I'll understand."

Why it's important to communicate

Although you see and hear all the time, chances are you're never absolutely sure what's really going on inside another person. At the most fundamental level, people are all human beings and probably much more alike than different, yet the gulf between you and other people may often be frustrating. In one way, you feel that you know a person, but in another way, you're sure you don't. And knowing other people is important at times.

Understanding means effectiveness

The better your understanding of another person, the more effective you can be in terms of managing him or her.

Communication promotes understanding

This is where communication skills become important add-ons. When you choose to use these skills, you can find out a great deal more about where individuals are. You can add to your understanding and action in ways that will help you defuse tension, decrease the chances of trouble, and increase your ability to handle any and all situations more effectively. The basic skills covered in Section I let you size up the situation. The add-on communication skills presented in this section help you understand the full implications of that situation and act constructively.

WHAT ARE THE SKILLS? Once you choose to communicate, you begin by putting all of the five basic skills to use: arranging, positioning, posturing, observing, and listening. As the process of communicating develops, you use new skills in two important ways.

The two skills
- Responding to people
- Asking relevant questions

As the materials that follow make clear, responding to people means a good deal more than just answering a greeting—although this, too, can be important. You need to take the initiative in developing effective responses. By the same token, asking relevant questions means more than a simple "Hey, what's going on?" Here in Section II, you'll have a chance to learn the specific procedures involved in responding and asking questions effectively.

GET READY BY USING THE BASICS As noted, communicating must begin with your use of all the basic skills. You arrange your environment to eliminate distractions and make it pleasant. You position yourself at the best possible distance—say three to four feet—when you are talking with a single person. This puts you close enough to see and hear everything, yet not so close that you seem overly threatening. You face the individual squarely, your left shoulder squared with his right and your right with his left. And you look directly at him, making appropriate eye contact to let him know you're really "right there."

You arrange your environment so that you can really focus on the person talking. You position yourself to communicate both confidence and real attention. You observe the appearance and behavior, using visual cues to draw inferences about feelings, the relationship with you, and general energy level. You listen carefully, making sure you take in all the key words and verbal indications of intensity so that you can determine just what a person's need really is. Only after you have really mastered and put to use the basic skills will you be able to use the add-on communication skills effectively.

Like the basic skills, the add-on skills involve a step-by-step approach. First you respond to the person. Then you ask any relevant questions you need to ask. Then you respond again, this time to the answers. You would usually not, in other words, just jump in and start asking questions—at least not if your goal is to get the person to open up and communicate useful information voluntarily. There may be times when the circumstances warrant using more forceful tactics. However, we do not have to teach force, and force always contains significant risk.

PRACTICE Think of managers you have worked for who were better at communicating than other supervisors. What qualities or skills did these good communicators have that made them effective? List two.

1) _____

_____

2) _____

_____

Responding

Responding means just that—showing a clear reaction to something that you have seen or heard. A response **gives evidence** that you have listened. In this section, we'll take a look at several levels of responding. At the simplest level, you can respond to content by summarizing and expressing what a person or group of people has said or done. At the next level, you can respond to the feelings shown in a person's words or reflected in his actions, particular feelings, and the reasons for those feelings.

There are three levels of responding:

THE ADD-ONS

Communicating with People

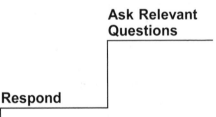

**Ask Relevant
Questions**

Respond

1. Responding to content
2. Responding to feeling
3. Responding to feeling
   and meaning

Each new level of responding does more to show a person that you are really on top of things—really seeing, hearing, and understanding him or her in terms of where he or she is. Probably more than anything else in this training, responding is going to seem strange to you. It's new and you may be doubtful about its worth. There are some things to remember here:

1) We are not telling you that you can't use other communications techniques that have worked for you in the past.

2) We are trying to "add-on" to techniques you may already have to increase your communication abilities.

3) The more techniques you have to handle a given situation in life, the greater your chances of success or control of the outcome. Techniques are like tools in a toolbox: the more you have and know how to use them, the greater chance you can fix a problem.

Responding to content. Responding to content is the skill of seeing and hearing what is really happening and the ability to reflect that understanding back to a person. You're letting a person know that you heard accurately and are on top of the situation.

While your use of the basic skills establishes a relationship in which people are more likely to cooperate with and talk to you, responding is a tool you can use spontaneously to communicate with anyone. Responding to content is the first part of effective responding. It shows a person that you have heard or seen what he or she said or did. When any person, including those you must manage, knows that you are seeing and/or hearing him or her accurately, he or she will tend to talk more freely. This is critical because talking not only gives you more of the information you need, it also allows people to get things off their chest.

There are two steps to responding to content: a) reflecting on what was seen and heard, and b) using the responding format to respond to content.

Ask Relevant Questions

Respond

1. Responding to content
   a) Reflect on what was
      seen and heard
   b) Use responding format
      to respond to content

Use the basics When responding to content, you are focused on what people are either saying or doing. Using what you have learned, you focus by arranging your environment, and posturing and positioning yourself for observing and/or listening to the person.

Reflect on what was seen and heard Next, you reflect on what you have seen and heard: "What is he doing?" and "What is he saying?" "How does he look?" In answering these questions, stick close to what is actually going on and/or what is being said.

Use responding format Finally, after taking it all in and reflecting on it, you summarize what the people are saying or doing in your own words. You respond to the content by saying to a person either:

"You look (it looks) _____" or

"You're saying _____."

For example: "You **look** pretty busy" or "You're **saying you're** pretty busy."

You respond to content when you want more information to aid you in management. You may do this when you are interviewing or when you notice unusual behavior in a person or group of people and would like to get some information

44

from them about what they are doing. For example, you might notice a group of unusually talkative supervisees being very quiet. You could say to them: "You are all pretty quiet today." This gives them the opportunity to respond to you while also letting them know that you are observing them and observing them accurately. Unlike other approaches designed to get information, responding to content doesn't automatically put people on the defensive.

RESPONDING at the simplest
level reflects content:

"You're saying _____."

PRACTICE   List two examples of situations in which you might respond to content in order to get more information from a supervisee.

1) _____

2) _____

List two reasons why you might want to get involved with a supervisee.

1) _____

2) _____

Example   Here's an example. You are in your office talking with two supervisees (a male and a female) who aren't getting along. You "position" yourself out from behind your desk and place their chairs so that you are at an appropriate distance, facing them squarely and looking directly at them. You "posture" yourself so that they know they've got your full attention.

You instruct the supervisees on your ground rules. Only one person talks at a time. The female supervisee speaks, "He is always telling me he'll handle situations that he believes I shouldn't have to handle because I'm a female. He tells me based on his experience that females can't handle certain situations."

You respond, "So you're telling me he's not letting you handle situations he believes should not be handled by females based on his experience." She says, "That's right."

You ask the male supervisee to tell you his side. "Well I had this other female co-worker and there were situations I didn't think she should have to manage, and she had no problem with that." You respond, "So you believe that based on your prior experience with a female co-worker, you know what's best for your current female co-worker." The male supervisee says, "Yes."

VIDEO **"Responding to Content: The Wrong Way and the Right Way"**

46

Supervisee	Manager	Group
1) Gives the setting 2) Role plays	1) Positions Postures Observes Listens 2) Waits 30 seconds 3) Gives responses: "You're saying _____." "You look (it looks) _____."	1) Positions Postures Observes Listens 2) Writes own responses 3) Rates manager's response. "Yes," if accurate, "No," if not, plus reason

Get people to talk instead of act

Supervisees can sometimes experience anxiety when they encounter managers. Of course, if you are the supervisee who has summoned assistance, the typical impact upon observing the responding manager will be a reduction of your anxiety. Of course, if you think you have done something wrong or you are going to be critiqued by a manager, your anxiety is likely to increase.

When supervising people who have anxiety, it's a good idea to let people talk off some of their anxiety rather than for them to act it out. Responding will assist greatly in accomplishing this.

Continuing with the above example, you observe the female supervisee's facial expression. Inferring that she's angry, you say, "You look (inference) annoyed." She responds, "I am annoyed because I know what I'm doing."

You are now setting the stage for the next responding skill: responding to feeling.

Responding to feeling. Responding to feeling is the ability to capture in words the specific feeling experience being presented by a person. By responding to, or reflecting back, the person's feeling, you show that you understand that feeling. This encourages the person to talk—to release his or her feelings.

The two steps in responding to feeling are a) reflect on feeling, and b) reflect on feeling and intensity.

**Ask Relevant
Questions**

Respond

1. Responding to content
2. Responding to feeling
   a) Reflect on feeling
   b) Reflect on feeling and
      intensity

Every supervisee has feelings that affect what they say and do. The nature and strength of these feelings usually determine what a supervisee is going to do. When you respond to a supervisee's feelings, you are encouraging him or her to talk. The skill of responding to feelings has important implications for the management of supervisees.

RESPONDING at the next level
reflects feelings:

"You feel _____."

Understanding can defuse bad feelings

Showing that you understand how a supervisee feels can be more powerful than showing that you understand the content of their actions and/or words. Showing a supervisee that you understand their negative feelings can usually **defuse** those negative feelings. By responding to feelings at the verbal or "symbolic" behavior level, you keep the person's words from turning to action. Also, responding to feelings at a verbal level can give you the necessary clues to determine the supervisee's intention. If she clams up after you have responded to her feelings, she may be telling you that she is going to act on them; on the other hand, if she goes with it verbally, she is telling you that she wants to talk it out instead of act on it.

Greater understanding

Besides being able to defuse negative feelings so that words don't become negative actions, responding to feelings leads to greater understanding of a supervisee. A supervisee can't always link up their feelings with the situation and is often at a loss to understand where they are. In addition, when you respond to positive feelings, these feelings get reinforced (unlike negative feelings). There's nothing mysterious about this. We don't enjoy our negative feelings, so we get rid of them by sharing them—by talking them out. But we do enjoy our positive feelings, so they only become stronger when they're shared with another person. You can choose to strengthen the positive feelings that will help a supervisee act more positively simply by recognizing and responding to these feelings. As a general rule, a person who feels positive about him- or herself will try to do positive things, while a person who feels negative about him- or herself will try to do negative things. If you expand on this, you arrive at the general principle: **People tend to act in ways consistent with the way other significant people see and act toward them.**

PRACTICE List two situations where it would be important and useful to defuse negative feelings of a supervisee.

1) _____

_____

2) _____

_____

Use the basics For responding to feeling, you position and posture yourself, then observe and listen. Then you reflect for the feeling (happy, angry, sad, scared) and its intensity (high, medium, or low).

Finally, you respond by saying:

"You feel _____ ."

For example, "You feel angry."

Reflect on feelings Here, the new skill involves reflecting for feeling and intensity. Adding a new skill doesn't mean discarding the old skills, of course. When reflecting for feeling, you are really asking yourself, "Given what I see and hear, how does this supervisee basically feel?" Is he happy, angry, sad, **Happy?** scared, or confused? This supervisee's behavior **Angry?** and words will let you make a good guess at the **Sad?** feeling. For example, a supervisee who shouts at **Scared?** another person, "You stupid idiot, now look what **Confused?** you've done!" while he shakes his fist and gets red in the face is obviously feeling a level of anger.

After you have picked out the feeling word, you must reflect on the intensity of the feeling. For example, anger can be high in intensity (mad), medium in intensity (annoyed), or low in intensity (bothered). The more accurate your feeling word reflects the intensity, the more effective your response will be. That is, your response will be more accurate and will do the job better (e.g., defuse the negative feeling). You wouldn't choose *concerned* for the above example because the term is too weak to describe a man yelling, shaking his fist, and turning red. Such an understatement would probably only make him more angry, but "You feel mad" would fit fine.

Take each of the five basic feeling words (happy, angry, confused, sad, and scared) and write a high, medium, and low intensity word for each.

FEELING WORDS

	High	Medium	Low
Happy	_____	_____	_____
Angry	_____	_____	_____
Confused	_____	_____	_____
Sad	_____	_____	_____
Scared	_____	_____	_____

"Responding to Feeling: The Wrong Way and the Right Way"

Below are some ground rules you should consider before the role-play activity:

1) People may not want to take responsibility for their emotions and deny they feel anything (don't pressure them).

2) People may correct you by expressing a feeling word that better describes how they feel (just let them).

3) The intensity of a person's feelings may be so high that they can't talk about them (so be patient and go back to your basic skills: arrange, position, posture, observe, listen).

ROLE-PLAY ACTIVITY

Supervisee	Manager	Group
1) Shares a real problem* **2)** Rates response after group rating	**1)** Positions Postures Observes Listens **2)** Pauses 10 to 20 seconds **3)** Responds, "You feel _____."	**1)** Positions Postures Observes Listens **2)** Writes own "You feel _____." **3)** Rates "Yes/No" on manager's response and why **4)** Gives individual response to group

Should not be anything that would be intimidating, embarrassing, or hurtful to self or others

Responding to feeling and meaning. Responding to feeling and meaning combines the two previous skills. It requires you to paraphrase the content of a supervisee's statement in such a way as to provide a meaningful reason for the person's feeling.

The two steps in responding to feeling and meaning are a) reflect on the feeling and the reason for that feeling and b) respond to the feeling and meaning.

**Ask Relevant
Questions**

Respond

1. Responding to content
2. Responding to feeling
3. Responding to feeling and meaning
    a) Reflect on feeling and reason
    b) Respond to feeling and meaning

**Reflect on
feeling and
reason** Learning how to respond to content and how to respond to feeling has prepared you to respond to feeling and meaning. Now your response at this new level can put everything together. Here you will capture effectively where the person is at the moment. By adding the meaning to the feeling, you will help yourself and the supervisee to understand the reason for his or her feelings about the situation. The reason is simply the personal meaning for the supervisee about what is happening.

Example Continuing with the example from the Responding to Content section, when you responded to the female supervisee, you said, **"You look annoyed."**

She responded: "I am annoyed because I know what I'm doing. I do not need my hand held. I know how to ask for help if I need it, so I need him (male supervisee) to stop assuming I need him to take over because a prior female co-worker let him."

You respond: "So you're **annoyed** (feeling) because he (male supervisee) assumes you need help just because a prior female co-worker needed help" (meaning).

She responds: "Yes, that's right! I appreciate his concern (male supervisee's) and I know he means well. I do value his experience in teaching me what I need to know" (female supervisee is feeling understood and her anger seems to be becoming less intense).

RESPONDING at the highest level
reflects both feeling and meaning.

"You feel _____ because _____."

By putting together the feeling and meaning in the above example and responding to both, you show a supervisee that you understand her experience as she presents it. This increases the chances of the supervisee talking to you about the thing in which you are interested. In addition, for supervision purposes, you will be able to learn more about what the supervisee values and what bothers her so that you can understand her and, if necessary, use the values and knowledge to apply pressure on the supervisee.

In another situation, a supervisee discusses a concern he has about his recent performance review:

Supervisee: I know I deserve better than an average score on my time management at work.

Supervisor: I know you are angry because I didn't think you deserved above-average rating on the time management.

Supervisee: That's right, I don't want it affecting my getting my normal merit increase in pay.

Supervisor: You're saying you're upset because it could affect your merit pay increase. I'm sorry I didn't discuss that with you and allowed you to assume it would affect your salary. It won't, unless your management of time doesn't improve between now and the next performance review.

Supervisee: I'm relieved, I need the money.

The supervisor understands clearly where the supervisee is in the situation and where he wants (or needs) to be, and is able to suggest a possible solution. This became possible because the supervisor was able to attach an understanding of meaning to the feelings of the supervisee.

Respond to feeling and meaning

By building on what you know, you add the reason to the feeling response you have just learned. Your new way of responding becomes "You feel _____ because _____."

What we need to focus on here, of course, is an individual's reason (personal meaning) for his or her feeling. Supplying the reason means that you must understand why what happened is important. You do this by rephrasing the content in your own words to capture that importance.

You are actually giving the reason for the feeling. In this way, you make the person's feeling clearer and more understandable.

It is also important to capture whether the person is seeing him- or herself as responsible or seeing someone else as being responsible. Your response should reflect where he or she sees the responsibility in the beginning, even though you may not agree. By doing this, you will have a better chance of getting the person to open up. You can always disagree when it becomes necessary and effective to do so. Remember, if you have this skill, you can choose to use it. If not, no choice.

PRACTICE   A female supervisee is having problems at home in her marriage. Her job performance reflects this. She says to you out of frustration, "You know, this job takes its toll on marriages and no one in this organization cares."

Identify the intensity and category of this feeling and pick an accurate "feeling" word to describe the person's emotion.

Feeling Word: _____

Now supply the reason for the supervisee's feeling. What does her situation really mean to her? Who is she blaming? Why is all of this so important to her? What does this mean to her? Put yourself in her place. Recognizing the meaning, formulate a response.

Response to Feeling and Meaning:

"You feel _____ because _____

_____

_____ ."

Example "You feel upset because you believe that this organization doesn't care how it affects an employee's marriage."

This response would probably surprise the supervisee. She probably expected the manager to deny everything—to tell her to grow up and ignore the whole thing. She certainly didn't expect the manager to respond to her situation at the same level that she was experiencing it.

Because the manager knew how to respond at this level, he/she was able to keep the supervisee talking openly. And in a tense situation, this can mean the difference between an effective supervisor and an ineffective manager.

Referral When responding to feeling and meaning, a communication interchange may sometimes go deeper than you feel you can handle. If this happens, you must consider the option of a **referral.** With your added understanding, your referral will be that much more specific and beneficial.

But many times, your added understanding will provide you with the information you need to really manage people. The payoff for you will be rewarding. Many supervisees put in their time, but don't get the payoff because they lack some of the skills needed to finish off the good start that they make by being decent and fair. Responding is one way to ensure the payoff.

Practice your responding skills with supervisees with whom you have been communicating. When you practice the skill, don't just give one response and say to yourself, "Well, I did it." Keep using your responding skills over and over again when you choose to understand. When you feel they have said all they are going to say, or when you know all you need to know, then you can take action.

But be careful about giving advice or getting involved. A lot of times, a person will hold back until he or she sees how you react. If you tell the person what to do or become overly involved, you may be placing yourself in either a vulnerable situation or one over your head.

VIDEO | **"Responding to Feeling and Meaning: The Wrong Way and the Right Way"**

ROLE-PLAY ACTIVITY

Supervisee	Manager	Group
1) Gives real stimulus	**1)** Positions Postures Observes Listens	**1)** Positions Postures Observes Listens
2) Gives spontaneous reply following each response	**2)** Pauses 10 to 20 seconds	**2)** Writes own response to feeling and meaning
3) Rates responder after group rating	**3)** Gives response: "You feel _____."	**3)** Rates "Yes/No" on last response. If not, why?
	4) Pauses 10 to 20 seconds	**4)** Gives individual response to group
	5) Gives response: "You feel _____ because _____."	**5)** Gives feedback on sizing up

Asking Questions

You ask questions in order to get useful answers. Some questions get better answers than others: the skill of asking questions will help you increase your information base and hence your ability to manage others.

The two steps in asking questions are:

INTERVENTION MODEL

THE ADD-ONS

Communicating with People

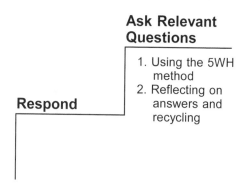

Ask Relevant Questions

1. Using the 5WH method
2. Reflecting on answers and recycling

Respond

TWO STEPS IN ASKING QUESTIONS As the following materials make clear, there are really two basic steps involved in asking relevant questions in an effective way. Having responded to a person at the most accurate level, you must develop one or more **questions of the 5WH** type: Who, What, Where, When, Why and How. And second, you must **reflect** on the answer or answers given by the person to make sure you fully understand all the implications. Did you get the information you wanted? Was new information revealed?

Asking questions will help you manage. If people answered our questions satisfactorily, we would be all set. After all, we have all the right questions. The reality, however, is that for a variety of reasons (e.g., lack of trust, guilt), many people do not answer questions fully or accurately. In fact, questions will sometimes have the opposite effect. That is, they will shut off communication with people rather than open it up. This is because questions are often seen as the bullets of the enemy ("Cover up, here they come"). The only way questions can be really effective in getting a person to open up is when they are used *in addition to* the basic skills plus responding. Use of the basics plus responding can get a person to the point where they will talk quite openly. It is then that questions can make their contribution by getting some of the necessary specifics (who, what, when, where, why, and how—the 5WH system).

Use the basics plus responding

PART 1 OF ASKING QUESTIONS

Asking 5WH questions. Answers to questions will give you the detail you need to manage people effectively. The more details you know, the better you can understand what is going on. You always want to know **who** is involved, **what** they are doing or going to do, **when** and **where** something happened or will happen, **how** it's going to be done or how it was done, and **why** it did or will take place.

> "Where were you?"
> "Who were you with?"
> "Why were you there?"
> "What did you actually do?"
> "When did all this happen?"
> "How was it handled?"

Respond, then ask

When you have all this information, you can take appropriate action and/or prevent problems from happening (now and maybe in the future). Question-asking can be used with responding during an interrogation, interview, or when you choose to assist with a problem.

Responding opens up the person and gives you a chance to make sure you understand what is being said. It also builds up trust with a person. For these reasons, you should always try to respond to a supervisee's actions or words at the highest possible level before you actually start asking questions. Questions then fill in the details of the picture. Often details (reasons) come from responding skills alone if you have patience. If they do not, questions are appropriate. It's as simple as that.

PRACTICE   For each of the following situations, first make a response and then ask an appropriate question.

1) A supervisee has been late to work three times in the past two weeks, but has not called in to let you know. He says: *"Look, I know this looks bad. I'm sorry, but I'd rather not talk about why I have been late."*

Respond: "You feel _____

because _____

_____ ."

Questions (5WH):   " _____

_____

_____

_____ ?"

2) A supervisee says the following to you: *"I don't think it's fair that other people in this organization don't get the same disciplinary action for the same offense. It doesn't make any sense. It's not right!"*

Respond: "_____

_____ ."

Questions (5WH): "_____

_____

_____

_____ ?"

PART 2 OF ASKING QUESTIONS

Reflecting on answers to questions. It's not enough just to ask good questions. You also have to be able to make sense out of the answers you get (and recognize as well, perhaps, the answers you're still not getting). Begin by responding to the answer: "You're saying _____" or "So you feel _____." Then **reflect** on (observe and listen) or think carefully about the answer to your question.

The person may be leveling with you and giving you the information you need to manage things or even to provide assistance. This person may be leveling with you as best as he or she can, but perhaps not giving you all the information you need. Or this person may be covering up something, which means that he or she is still not fully open—still not really communicating with you. Your **observation** skills are critical here.

REFLECTING means thinking about
what you have—and haven't—learned.

How does she look?	When reflecting on the person's answer to your question, you can think about four specific things: How she looks as she answers (relaxed, uncomfortable); what she is doing while she answers (facing you and making eye contact, looking away, looking down at her feet); what she has actually said (the information content of her answer); and what she may have failed to say (any "gaps" in the way she answers). By reflecting on these four areas of concern, you can make sure that you fully understand all the implications of the answer. Once you've responded to this answer, you can ask additional questions to get the rest of the information you need. By using your basics—responding, asking good questions, reflecting, and then responding again—you'll be recycling.
What is she doing?	
What did she say?	
What didn't she say?	
Recycling	

Example A supervisee who has a reputation for being shy and quiet has recently lost his temper with another employee. He made some statements that were threatening to the other employee (at least from that employee's perspective).

A couple of witnesses to the incident have told you in private that the employee who was threatened has been provoking this supervisee by playing practical jokes on him.

As you talk to this supervisee in your office, he really doesn't say much (three- to five-word answers). He never mentions the other employee agitating him and playing practical jokes. In the end, his answers to your questions give you nothing.

Upon reflection, you realize that this supervisee is not only scared in general, but is really frightened right now. In other words, your reflecting skills let you know that this isn't a guy who's trying to play it smart with you. He's not clamming up on purpose. Instead, he's just living in fear right there in front of you.

Realizing all of this, you're able to respond even more fully and immediately to him: "You're scared stiff right now because you are afraid you are going to lose your job if you tell me you lost your temper. What has this person (other employee) done that may have caused you to lose your temper?"

The supervisee looks up, surprised. He didn't know any manager could really see and hear him as he actually is. You've just grown about six inches in his eyes—maybe to the point where you suddenly seem stronger than the threat of losing his job. Instead of clamming up, the supervisee keeps on talking, answering your next questions more fully. This is just what you want him to do, because in the end, you know you gained his confidence and learned the information you needed to get.

VIDEO **"Asking Relevant Questions: The Wrong Way and the Right Way"**

ROLE-PLAY ACTIVITY

Supervisee	Manager	Group
1) Role plays stimulus **2)** Reacts to responses and answers questions **3)** Gives feedback	**1)** Positions Postures Observes Listens **2)** Pauses and responds to feeling and/or meaning **3)** Asks questions after responding (5WH) **4)** Pauses and reflects on answer to question	**1)** Positions Postures Observes Listens **2)** Writes own responses and questions **3)** Rates manager's response **4)** Rates question "Yes/No" **5)** Presents each response and question **6)** Gives feedback on sizing up **7)** Reflects on choice of response: Would it have warranted both feeling and meaning?

Summary of the Add-Ons

Example Susan Brown is a new employee and is under the supervision of Ron Jones, a supervisor you manage.

There have been rumors floating that Ron has been saying inappropriate things of a sexual nature to Susan. It is also rumored that she's told a couple of other employees that she won't say anything; she is on her probationary period and doesn't want to lose her job if she complains.

Ron has been accused of this behavior in the past, but there was never sufficient information to substantiate it, so nothing ever happened.

You decided to talk with Susan about this because you don't tolerate sexual harassment. You're also concerned because this is the third instance where it has been rumored that Ron Jones may have a problem.

You ask Susan to meet with you. After a few social pleasantries, you have the following conversation:

You: How is the job going?

Susan: Everything is fine. I love working here.

You: How do you like working with Ron?

Susan: Oh, It's okay. He's alright.

You reflect on her answer and notice by her facial expression and voice tone that she was uneasy with her answer.

You: You seem a little apprehensive in your answer. Is everything okay?

Susan: Oh, I'm fine. Look, I don't want any trouble.

You: You seem scared because you want to tell me something you're uncomfortable about. What makes you uncomfortable?

After a half-hour interview, she tells you about three instances where Ron Jones has said inappropriate things.

In the first section of this manual, you learned the skills you need to size up a situation. Now, working through this second section, you've learned the skills you need in order to initiate meaningful communication to improve your management potential—the skills involved in responding and asking questions. These skills are designed to help you manage by using communication skills. The payoffs are always good for all concerned. Now it's time to move on—to go beyond sizing up and communicating and consider what's involved in really controlling the situation. We'll concentrate on this topic and the skills it requires in the final section of this manual.

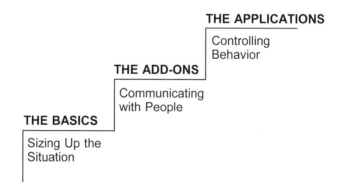

THE APPLICATIONS

Controlling Behavior

THE ADD-ONS

Communicating with People

THE BASICS

Sizing Up the Situation

Section III

The Applications:
Controlling Behavior

The application skills combine the basic and the add-on skills, and are aimed at controlling behavior. These skills are important in helping you maintain control and manage people well.

The applications include three specific skills:

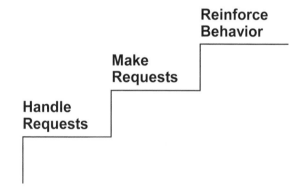

INTERVENTION MODEL

THE APPLICATIONS

Controlling Behavior

Reinforce Behavior

Make Requests

Handle Requests

Example   Manager Dave Johnson has a reputation for applying the rules when they suit him and always saying *"No"* just because he feels like it.

Dave has been married to his wife June for 20 years. Both of their children moved out of the house following high school. June informed Dave that she wanted a divorce, now that the children are gone. She told Dave their marriage for the most part was a failure due to Dave's over-controlling nature and his know-it-all attitude toward her and the children. Dave was shocked because he knew they had problems, but not to the point of divorce.

One evening, Dave was drinking at his favorite bar. He was feeling down; June had just moved out, leaving him alone in the house. Dave, knowing that he had had too much to drink, called three friends for a ride home. All three of them said they were busy and for him to take a cab.

Dave became angry after the third friend told him no. Dave decided to drive his vehicle home despite having a few drinks.

Approximately 5 minutes from home, he was stopped by a female state trooper. Dave got out of his car and identified himself as a contributor to the Police Benevolent Fund and an auxiliary police officer. Dave was expecting "officer courtesy" from what he perceived as a fellow officer.

The trooper wanted to see proof of insurance and Dave's driver's license. Dave refused, stating who he was. The trooper was young and "by the book." She told Dave she didn't care who he was. Dave became irate, and a heated argument ensued between him and the trooper. He refused to give the trooper his license and proof of insurance.

Eventually some backup troopers arrived and Dave was booked for DUI and placed in the county lockup. He was also charged with resisting arrest.

The moral of this story is not that Dave should have been given officer courtesy, but that Dave's management style of people had been arbitrary his whole life. Yet when Dave experienced someone like himself, he became angry and combative. If Dave had developed effective social intelligence skills earlier in his career, he might have prevented the above situation. He also might have preserved his marriage and family. Dave's poor controlling skills of himself and others led to his demise.

Controlling is the Key   Controlling behavior simply means taking charge when circumstances give no other options. Without the ability to control behavior, all the other efforts are wasted. A manager has to do everything he or she can to ensure appropriate behavior—in the interests of the organization and of supervisees. The same holds true for all of us. Learning to control our behavior is in our interest. Without control, nothing productive can or will occur.

This section of the manual builds on previous sections. It is about the "hows" of controlling behavior by using good management skills.

WHAT ARE THE SKILLS?   In this final section of the manual, we'll take a close look at three different controlling skills. These skills are called the applications because they really represent the specific ways in which you should apply all of the other skills you've developed in order to manage and control behavior along with these three controlling skills:

Three application skills

- Handling requests
- Making requests
- Reinforcing behavior

Unlike the earlier skills in Sections I and II, these three areas are not always cumulative—that is, you will be involved at any given time in either handling requests or making requests of your own. In either situation, however, you will want to reinforce the behavior—positively if you want someone to keep doing a particular thing, and negatively if you want to keep them from not doing something.

Before going any further, let's take a look at a couple of these skills in action.

Example   Here is a routine situation where a manager demonstrates skill in management. It could be handled much differently with more negative outcomes. It involves the manager making and handling a request and, in turn, a request being handled by the supervisee.

Manager Joan Wilson: Larry, I'd like you to switch your shift with Paul for the next two weeks because Paul has been having problems with his neck and can't drive.

Supervisee Larry Wright: Is it okay with you if I try to get someone else to do it? I'd like to keep my schedule since I started bowling in a league.

Manager Joan Wilson: I'm sorry, Larry, I know that would upset your schedule, but I can't use anyone else since you are the only one who can switch in your unit. I've already checked it out with the other guys. It will only be until Paul's neck gets better.

Supervisee Larry Wright: Why do you always pick on me? I'm always the one who gets screwed on these deals.

Manager Joan Wilson: I know this irritates the heck out of you because it will interrupt your routine, but it's the best I can do right now. Please report at 10:00 a.m. tomorrow instead of 2:00 p.m.

Control through skill The manager in this case used her skills to control the situation. She didn't demean or put down, and she didn't use sarcasm. You will observe, however, that included in her skills were firmness and reasons for her actions. There was no weakness. The supervisee now knows what he is expected to do and why. The manager was even able to continue to be responsive to the supervisee when he became irritated. The use of skill gets the job done and increases the probability that the supervisee will feel he has been treated fairly even if he has to have his routine interrupted.

PRACTICE Why is control important for management?

_____

_____

_____

What does a supervisee gain when they learn to control their own behavior?

_____

_____

_____

Handling Requests

Handling requests is the ability to manage requests of others in a fair and effective manner. The skillful handling of requests helps build trust and reduce tension.

The two steps in handling requests are:

INTERVENTION MODEL

THE APPLICATIONS

Controlling Behavior

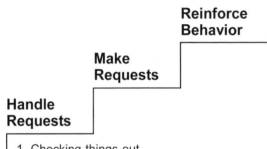

Reinforce Behavior

Make Requests

Handle Requests

1. Checking things out
2. Giving response and reason

Rules, regulations, and rights

Before we turn to the skills involved in handling requests, we should review the way in which rules and regulations often relate to the specific things to which people do and do not have a right to do.

A manager is bound by certain legal and departmental requirements to provide certain things to supervisees. Most of these things are seen to be basic rights and/or needs to which all supervisees are entitled. You as a manager have probably written regulations to guide you in these areas. Abiding by these rights and needs usually enables a manager to establish a working relationship with most supervisees that is objective and not personal.

There is always that 10 to 20 percent who react negatively no matter what you do. But by following the regulations, you can expect people to do what is expected. You have taken away excuses for negative behavior, even in the eyes of the people who want to see you as unfair or arbitrary.

PART 1 OF HANDLING REQUESTS **Checking out the person and situation.** While responding to any request, you need to use your basic skills to check out the person who makes it. Is this person leveling with you, or is he or she trying to play some kind of game? You also need to check out the situation in terms of any policies or regulations that might apply. Using your positioning, observing, listening, and responding skills will be invaluable to you here. As you practice, this will become very clear to you.

CHECKING THINGS OUT involves
sizing up the person and/or situation.

Legitimate or Not? It goes without saying that as a manager you will receive requests from people. Some will be legitimate, some not. Each request must be responded to. Even if you ignore a request, you have responded to it, and some consequence will occur that can affect your ability to handle and control people. If you find this hard to believe, put yourself in a situation where you want your supervisor to consider a request of your own and he or she ignores you.

1) How might you feel if a request was important to you and it was denied?

Feeling word: _____

2) What message would it communicate if it happened often?

_____

_____

3) How might it affect your performance?

_____

_____

CHECKING OUT REQUESTS
involves deciding if the requests
are legitimate or not.

Sometimes there will be situations where circumstances cannot be handled by regulations or rules. They may require the following questions to be asked before granting or not granting a request:

- Does a basic need/right apply to the request (beyond policy and procedure)?

  Example: *The supervisee must deal with a life or death emergency.*

- Does the supervisee's special circumstances or past performance apply to the request?

  Example: *The supervisee has a history of doing good work and rarely makes requests that could override rules and regulations.*

- Are there situational circumstances beyond rules and regulations that might apply to granting or not granting the request?

  Example: *If you force the application of the rules or regulations, you make matters worse for everyone concerned (you, the requestor, and the organization as a whole).*

Keep in mind Rules and regulations are necessary because they provide guidelines for everyone to follow without personal emotions or perceptions affecting the request response.

On the other hand, the application of rules and regulations has the potential for making matters worse. This is because rules and regulations cannot list every exception to the rule or predict circumstances that require flexibility.

Also keep in mind that as a manager, if you circumvent a rule or regulation that causes a bigger problem, you are accountable.

PRACTICE Read the following situations, then describe how you would check them out.

Supervisee request: "Donna, can I leave early today to pick up my child? My wife can't do it."

What skills would be important to use in this situation?

_____

_____

What rules or regulations must be considered?

_____

_____

Female supervisee request: "Jim Garner said something to me in the hallway that I thought was rude. I don't think he has a right to talk to me like that. I want you to do something about it now, or I will go over your head."

What skills would be important to use in this situation?

_____

_____

What rules or regulations must be considered?

_____

_____

By knowing which of the sizing-up and communicating skills to use, you can ensure that you really know what's happening with a particular person who has a request. And by reviewing the appropriate rules and regulations, you'll have a good idea of whether the request is or is not legitimate.

Check Things Out: Summary To summarize, when checking things out:

1) Use basic skills: arrange, position, posture, observe, listen.

2) Use add-ons if applicable: respond and ask relevant questions.

3) Know policies and procedures that apply to the request.

4) Ask: Does a basic need/right apply to the request?

5) Ask: Does the supervisee's special circumstances or past performance apply to the request?

6) Ask: Are there situational factors that apply to the request?

Now you're ready to respond to the request itself.

Responding with a reason for your decision.
This skill involves indicating the action you're going to take—your decision—and giving the person your reason. Giving the supervisee a good reason is not a sign of weakness. On the contrary, it is the best way in which to minimize future gripes. If you turn the supervisee down, he or she won't be able to complain that you didn't even say why. And if you grant the supervisee's request, he or she will know that it was for a good and clear reason.

RESPONDING with a reason
eliminates possible hassles.

Reasons for action

Basically, a manager has three possible avenues of action in relation to a request. In each case, the manager should give some reason for his or her action. Here are some formats that can be used:

"Yes" "Yes, I'll do (it) _____ because _____."

"No" "No, I won't do (it) _____ because _____."

"I'll check" "I'll look into (it) _____ because _____ and I will get back to you (when) _____ and (where) _____ with the answer."

How you decide

In each instance, the manager bases his or her intent on the rules and regulations that apply. In cases where people need or request something beyond what they are entitled to by rules and regulations (discussed previously), each person's behavior (past and present), what is asked for, the way it is asked for, and other information you have gained by checking things out may determine your response. For example, a supervisee's spouse asks you, "Can you tell me if my wife is working extra hours? She says she's working overtime and that's why she's not coming home." As her manager, you know she hasn't been working overtime, but you deny the request because this is a personal matter.

Take care of basic rights While a manager may have an option in a case like the above, some things—like responding to a supervisee's husband in distress—can be denied. You may not have options for a supervisee who claims sexual harassment and demands separation from the harasser even if you have no proof. Knowing the rules and the regulations of your organization will definitely make your job easier; by taking care of the basic rights/needs of supervisees, tensions in the workplace will be greatly reduced.

PRACTICE List four legitimate requests a supervisee could make in your organization:

1) _____

2) _____

3) _____

4) _____

List four non-legitimate requests a supervisee could make in your organization:

Request	**Why**
1) _____	_____
2) _____	_____
3) _____	_____
4) _____	_____

List four "maybe" requests a supervisee could make in your organization:

	Request	Why
1)	_____	_____
2)	_____	_____
3)	_____	_____
4)	_____	_____

VIDEO

"Handling Requests: The Wrong Way and the Right Way"

ROLE-PLAY ACTIVITIY

Supervisee	Manager	Group
1) Gives the setting **2)** Makes requests **3)** Gives feedback after group has finished their assignment	**1)** Positions Postures Observes Listens **2)** Checks things out— responds, asks relevant questions **3)** Pauses 30 seconds to assess request (legitimate or not) **4)** Gives action plus reason	**1)** Positions Postures Observes Listens **2)** Checks things out **3)** Rates manager: a) action plus reason, "Yes/No"; b) action and reason. If "no," why? **4)** Gives action plus response for feedback

PRACTICE   List four non-legitimate requests a supervisee would make to practice the above:

1) _____

2) _____

3) _____

4) _____

Making Requests

Making requests is the ability to manage people by making specific requests of them. Making requests skillfully improves the chances that they will cooperate and more readily carry out your requests.

The two steps in making requests are:

THE APPLICATIONS

Controlling Behavior

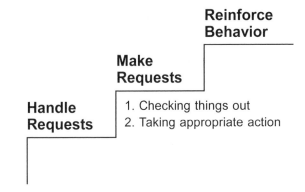

Reinforce Behavior

Make Requests

Handle Requests

1. Checking things out
2. Taking appropriate action

The two procedures involved in making requests in an effective way are checking things out (using the same procedures as when you are handling requests) and taking appropriate action. As before, you need to check things out to ensure that you don't make the wrong move—a move that might increase tension rather than calm things down. Once you've done this, you can decide whether the best action will involve a simple request, an order, or even direct physical action.

Checking things out. Since the procedures here will be the same as those involved in handling requests, there's no need to go back over them at length. Here, however, your aim should be to understand as much as possible about the situation involving the person you plan to have do something: Are they with family members/ friends? Are they someone you've had prior problems with? Will they feel they're losing face if you give them some direction, and therefore react antagonistically? Are they in the midst of doing something already and you will be interrupting them? By using your basic sizing-up and responding skills, increase the chances that you will make a request that a person or people will respond to without increasing tension.

Know the situation

Use basic skills

CHECKING THINGS OUT involves
the use of your basic and responding skills and
skills applicable to handling requests.

Taking appropriate action. Making requests of supervisees is obviously a routine part of supervising people. Many requests are made and often little thought is given to the impact of requests both on the control of supervisees and their immediate and long-term cooperation. Yet it is *how* the request is made that often makes the difference, not the nature of the request.

TAKING ACTION means selecting
the best way to make your request.

How you ask
may mean
more than
what you ask

In taking action to get a supervisee to do something, you have to be specific. You should identify what you want done and when. Telling a supervisee in this manner keeps you clear. You've put it right out there for them and anybody else to see. Many managers have found that a polite request is effective in getting a supervisee to do what they are told.

Of course, there are managers who feel that supervisees don't deserve politeness or that being polite makes a manager look weak. But you were brought up with good manners, and the question is, are you going to let a supervisee who is not being polite bring you down to his or her level? In addition, when a supervisee doesn't do something reasonable when asked politely, then it is he or she who looks weak and not you. Moreover, by being initially polite, you've given the supervisee the opportunity to go the "easy way." Now it's his or her responsibility if you have to go the "hard way."

It may be difficult to use a polite format, but many managers have found that it is more effective to be polite. It gets the results you want.

Mild or polite format
A mild (polite) request can take the form: "Would you (please) _____" or it can take the form "I would appreciate it if you would _____."

Direct format
When you make a request, the most direct method is simply to identify what you desire and then use the format "I want you to _____."
But because people often resent authority if you are simply telling them to do something, you may have fewer hassles if you use more of a polite/mild request format. Examples might be "I'd like you to do _____" or "Would you stop _____?"

Softening a request
You can soften the statement even more by using polite words, for example, "I'd like you to *please* stop _____." What format you use for making a request will depend on the situation and the particular supervisee. Of course, if a person abuses the mild method, you are always free to move to a stronger position, including a direct order. As indicated above, the point is to get the

Get stronger when necessary

job done—to have the person do what you want. Most experienced managers agree that over time, it is generally better if direct confrontation can be avoided.

Making Request Formats

Mild: "Would you (request) because (reason)."

Moderate: "I want you to (request) because (reason)."

Strong
(Immediate
Action): "I want you to (request) now."

Use responding skills

You may want to use your basic and responding skills in making requests. For example, you come across a supervisee who is in a place where he should not be. You **position** yourself so that you can see him, but he cannot see you. You **observe** for a little while because he appears to be doing nothing wrong. Then you move into **position** so that he can also see you. As you approach, you recognize the person. He in fact gives you a greeting: "Hello." You give him the benefit of the doubt in the sense that you are open to what he is going to say. The person is a new employee to the area and you haven't seen or heard anything to make you more than routinely cautious. You make your request:

Manager:
(Moderate) Hi! This is a restricted area. You'll have to leave it right now.

New
Supervisee: I just wanted to get off by myself for a while.

Manager: I can appreciate your wanting
(Softening by some privacy, but you can't be in
responding) this area without authorization.

PRACTICE There may be times when you want to start right out with a direct order or take immediate action as in the above. List two examples when you would give a direct order or take immediate action in your organization without making a request. Give the reason why you would do this.

Direct Order

Situation 1: _____

_____

Situation 2: _____

_____

Take Immediate Action

Situation 1: _____

_____

Situation 2: _____

VIDEO **"Making Requests: The Wrong Way and the Right Way"**

ROLE-PLAY ACTIVITY	Supervisee	Manager	Group
	1) Says "no" to the request and refuses to give a reason **2)** Argues	**1)** Positions Postures **2)** Makes a legitimate request of the supervisee **3)** Checks things out: Observes Listens Responds Asks questions **4)** Escalates the request; makes it more directive	**1)** Positions Postures Observes Listens **2)** Records own version of request and why it should be made **3)** Rates manager "Yes/No" on content and style of request, then gives own version of request

Reinforcing Behavior

We reinforce desirable behaviors that we want to keep occurring or occur more often, and we punish undesirable behaviors that we want to occur less often, or maybe not at all.

The four steps of reinforcing behavior are:

THE APPLICATIONS

Controlling Behavior

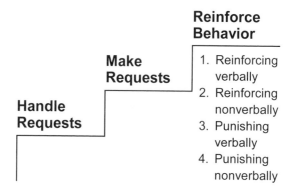

Reinforce Behavior

Make Requests

Handle Requests

1. Reinforcing verbally
2. Reinforcing nonverbally
3. Punishing verbally
4. Punishing nonverbally

In general, people perform behaviors that give them a good feeling, and they typically avoid behaviors that make them feel uncomfortable. The problem is that we often experience those good feelings (i.e., feel rewarded) for behaviors that are undesirable or inappropriate. For example, criminals who go uncaught are reinforced by the attention and material gain. Parents often reinforce complaining children in grocery stores by giving them sweets. Some managers receive the adulation of their peers for their use of force. In these examples, the rewards that accompany the criminal behavior, the public complaining, and the use of force almost certainly guarantee that these behaviors will continue and maybe increase in frequency.

Being a supervisor or manager means that you have the opportunity to change the behaviors of your supervisees using some fundamental skills of **reinforcing** those behaviors you want to maintain or increase and **punishing** those behaviors you want to decrease or eliminate. Using reinforcement and punishment appropriately can enhance the likelihood of responsible behavior from supervisees immediately while working toward long-term outcomes such as supervisee cooperation and support. **Note:** The better the rapport you have with the supervisee, the more efficient and effective your reinforcing and punishing will be in shaping his or her behavior.

Two kinds of reinforcement

Reinforcement refers to the use of rewards to maintain or increase desired behaviors. Reinforcement can be given by both verbal and nonverbal feedback to supervisees.

REINFORCING means using verbal and/or nonverbal responses as ways to maintain and/or increase desired behaviors

---

Verbal reinforcement

Verbal reinforcement means saying something with the intention of maintaining or increasing a desired behavior. Most of the time, the words we choose are experienced as pleasant by the person we're talking to. We've all heard or said these phrases: "Bob, thank you for always being prompt with your report," or "John, I appreciated you taking the responsibility for that without being asked," or " Sarah, great job!"

Unfortunately, we are probably also familiar with words or phrases that are *not* experienced as pleasant, but are still aimed at maintaining or increasing a desired behavior. For example, when a supervisee, Beth Williams, asked her supervisor if he got her shift report, he replied, "Of course I did. What are you looking for, a compliment?

That's your job." The manager's intent may have been to maintain or increase the behavior of completing an on-time shift report, but his response didn't leave the supervisee with a very pleasant feeling.

Which response would you prefer: "Great job with that shift report. Thanks!" or "That's your job!"

VIDEO **"Reinforcing Behavior Verbally: The Wrong Way and the Right Way"**

Nonverbal reinforcement Nonverbal reinforcement means using nonverbal cues to maintain or increase desired behaviors. The most obvious nonverbal cues are smiling, nodding the head, giving a pat on the back, etc. A person who cleans up her desk and gets a nod and a smile from her supervisor is an example of nonverbal reinforcement. Again, these are examples that will most likely leave the person with a pleasant feeling.

However, some nonverbal cues might be intended to reinforce a behavior, but actually might be experienced as less than pleasant. For example, let's look at Beth Williams from the above example. What if she had taken the complicated shift report on time to the manager and he snatched it out of her hands and placed it in his report basket while never making eye contact with her? His intent may have been to reinforce her on-time report writing by showing her what a busy man he is. If you were Beth Williams, what would you think?

VIDEO **"Reinforcing Behavior Nonverbally: The Wrong Way and the Right Way"**

Punishment Punishment means saying or doing something that is intended to reduce or eliminate an undesirable behavior. Again, this can be done using verbal and/or nonverbal feedback with supervisees.

Although it is generally accepted that punishment is a tool of "last resort" for the effective supervisor or manager, its timing is also determined by other factors, such as the nature of the behavior, the context in which the behavior occurred, previous displays of the behavior, and the rules and regulations that apply to the behavior, to name only a few. When administered fairly and appropriately, punishment can be a powerful way to change behaviors.

PUNISHMENT means using verbal and/or nonverbal responses as ways to decrease or eliminate undesirable behaviors.

Verbal punishment Verbal punishment means saying something with the intention of decreasing or eliminating an undesirable behavior. These can be some of your most difficult conversations. Therefore, your ability to size up the situation and use your responding and requesting skills will be invaluable here. And again, being polite can be your best asset. Examples of verbal punishments can be mild, such as "Please do not do that behavior again," or intense, "Stop it NOW!" They can express feelings, such as "I'm disappointed that you chose to behave that way," or they can be explanatory, "Let's talk about this behavior. You know, we've talked about this on two previous occasions, and now it's occurred again, so we're going to have to talk about the consequences of what you've done."

Not all verbal punishments involve spoken words. Making entries in a personnel file that document the behavior and its consequences also fit in this category.

Insults and hurtful statements are also examples of verbal punishment. "I can't believe you're so stupid that you are still writing that report. Grandma was slow, but she was old! Hurry up!" or "Only an idiot would try to do it that way."

Which of these verbal punishments would you prefer to receive if you had done something inappropriate—the mild statements or hurtful statements?

Nonverbal punishment Nonverbal punishment means using nonverbal cues to decrease or eliminate undesired behaviors. The most obvious nonverbal cues are shaking your head back and forth indicating "no" or "stop," looking at the person with a serious expression communicating displeasure, and rolling the eyes. Other nonverbal punishments involve removing privileges or assigning the person to undesirable duties.

Some of the less productive nonverbal punishments include slapping, hitting, punching, pinching, and other physically abusive behaviors. The use of obscene and/or exaggerated gestures of disgust, contempt, and displeasure are also considered generally ineffective.

PRACTICE List some verbal reinforcers you could give as a manager and the behaviors that would warrant them. (Remember that certain written statements are also included in this category, such as an entry into a supervisee's personnel file.)

Verbal reinforcers:

1) _____

2) _____

3) _____

4) _____

Behaviors receiving verbal reinforcers:

1) _____

2) _____

3) _____

4) _____

List some nonverbal reinforcers you can administer as a manager and the behaviors that would receive them.

Nonverbal reinforcers:

1) _____

2) _____

3) _____

4) _____

Behaviors receiving nonverbal reinforcers:

1) _____

2) _____

3) _____

4) _____

List some punishments you can administer as a manager and the behaviors that would warrant them:

Punishments:

1) _____

2) _____

3) _____

4) _____

Behaviors you might punish:

1) _____

2) _____

3) _____

4) _____

ROLE-PLAY ACTIVITY #1

Supervisee	Manager	Group
1) Gives the setting and trust level in existence **2)** Role plays a desired behavior (e.g., takes the lead on a project, turns in shift report complete and on-time, etc.)	**1)** Positions Postures Observes Listens **2)** Responds **3)** Reinforces desired behavior: a) Verbally b) Nonverbally	**1)** Responds Observes Listens **2)** Writes own reinforcement and why **3)** Rates manager "Yes/No" on correctness of reinforcement. If "No," why?

ROLE-PLAY ACTIVITY #2

Supervisee	Manager	Group
1) Role plays an undesired behavior (e.g., late for work, turns in shift report late and incomplete, etc.)	**1)** Positions Postures Observes Listens **2)** Responds **3)** Punishes undesired behavior: a) Verbally b) Nonverbally	**1)** Responds Observes Listens **2)** Writes own reinforcement and why **3)** Rates manager "Yes/No" on correctness of punishment. If "No," why?

Summary of the Applications

You've developed professional skills to do a professional's job. You've helped to lay to rest that familiar stereotype that supervisees have of the manager as being over-authoritarian, uncaring, and "bottom line" driven. And you've gone beyond: You've begun to act upon one of the most basic equations in all of human history.

HUMAN ACTIONS DETERMINE HUMAN REACTIONS
The cornerstone of the social intelligence skills you've learned is **decency:** simple human decency. You've got a job to do. But in doing it, you've learned how you can handle people like the human beings they are. And in return, you'll be able to promote more decent and constructive behavior on their part. This process involves what has been called "the principle of reciprocal behavior"—a fancy way of saying that **we all get back what we give**. In your case, you've learned how to invest your work with professional effectiveness—with real skills—and still give people decent treatment.

About the Author

Dr. Steve Sampson is the founder and president of SoTelligence®, Inc., which offers a series of courses, seminars, workshops, and intensives designed to teach people social and emotional intelligence and provide them with the skills necessary to develop, grow, and maintain healthy and rewarding personal relationships—at work, at home, and in their community.

Today, most training programs focus on teaching concepts that are of limited value when the participant leaves the classroom. Like many self-help books, these programs cover a lot, but they don't provide the attendee with the necessary "how to" instructions to accomplish the goals of the course.

At SoTelligence®, we employ a Tell-Show-Do-Feedback method of training where participants can learn about a concept, see it demonstrated by certified trainers, practice it in a safe and supportive environment, and receive (as well as give) feedback to others during practice rounds. This method has been shown to provide the best opportunity for participants to **develop new skills** and actually **change their behaviors**. For more information, contact us at www.SoTelligence.com.